20-10-2020

HORROR MEETS REALITY

A RECORD OF A TIME AND EVENTS SPOKEN IN EMOTIONS

A COLLECTION OF POEMS AND LYRIC ESSAYS

FON PETER

DEDICATION
20-10-2020

To all the souls lost

Before, during, and in the aftermath

To the heroic youth of our time

Those in the line of battle on and offline

To our parents and everyone else

As a lesson and example

To our children to come

Stories and a history for you…lessons

To Nigeria

On the Redemption Journey

We Move

We Heal

TABLE OF CONTENTS

20

BLEEDING STREETS

The streets will forever cry
The pain of our lost

The streets will forever echo
The footsteps of our fight

The streets will forever reflect
The power of our youth

The streets will forever burn
The heels of our killers

The streets will forever record
The transgressions of our leaders

The streets will forever rescue
The innocent from your hands

The streets will forever cry
The howls of the bereaved

The streets will forever cry
The tears of the broken all over

The streets will forever cry
The pain of our lost

The streets will forever remind
That one day comes for the owner

IGNORANCE PERISHES THE PEOPLE

The stupidity causing our demise
The ignorance of our torturers reasons
The foolishness of my assaulters logic
How dumb my accusers are!

Colored hair, printed skin
I've been labelled
Criminals, robbers, prostitutes
I've been labelled

I've been labelled
Because I expressed self through art
Art on my skin, art on my hair
I've been condemned

I've been labelled
Because I grew with the times
Because I evolved with the tech
I've been charged

I've been labelled
Because I've gotten my spoils after my toils
All still in my youth
I've been extorted

I've been labelled
By my fathers who sold me out
My fathers who have taken the baton of the enemies
I've been murdered

When will it stop?
Seeing as they do not know the tide changes
or they have chosen to refuse the reality before them
When will it stop?

I'll tell you when

When we take the blindfolds off,
off the clueless and archaic
When we force an enlightenment
on those who refuse the new reality

When the foolish murderer
gains exposure, gains an awakening
When education comes like a plague,
howling and tearing down all in its path

When education comes like the apocalypse;
Destroying everything and everyone amiss,
All and sundry who don't accept its mark
…and rebuilding a new world order of hope and better

For Ignorance perishes the people

THE OATH OF WAGES

Wages will always be accorded
In ways that surely can be afforded

In what ways, we do not know
But we are sure, will show

Blood will spill
The blood of the wicked

It always does
In time, no matter how long

The hand of vengeance will stretch out
By no prophecies or religion

But by the simple way of wages
The simple oath of karma

By the will and soul of the people
People who have been wronged

By the blood of the dead
Swimming in our rivers

Staining our sand
Nudging you to your deaths

Just like the tears of our fathers past
That pushed us sons to revolution fast

THE POLICEMEN WEPT

Men woke, believing in security
Or simply seeking a means of survival
Whichever was the case
and they ran to you

You offered them a hope
You offered them a home
You offered them a future
You offered them the opportunity for impact

Then you stifled their hearts
Strangled their purses
Castrated their legacies
Starved their kin

Then ordered them into crime
Making murderers of them
For your own murderous purposes
For your abominations

You made them the enemy
Now they are the haunted
And you, even in the throes
Still placed them at forefront of the fire's kiss

While their families sorrowed and hoped

Tearing their eyes into hopelessness
Each time they came home with nothing
Nothing to dine, nothing to wine

And the ones just like you
The ones you created…the ones you inspire
Became the beasts of the land with glee
After all, you've given them a why

And the honest ones… the humane ones
The ones without greed
Suffered silently in pain, protecting while they could
And crying while they sprayed your bullets

And while we watched, they wept
Wept through the pain, hopelessness, and starvation
And while we died, they wept
They wept through the crimes they committed

Shame
Hopelessness
Dehumanization
Inhumanity

The Policemen Wept

HAVE YOU KEPT US POOR?

Have you kept us poor
so that you can use us?
Have you kept us poor
so that we might be weak?

Have you kept us poor
so that education may not enlighten us?
Have you kept us poor
so that hunger will blind us?

Have you kept us poor?
so that choices will elude us
Have you kept us poor?
so that chaos may befriend us?

Have you kept us poor
so that time and pain may ready us?
Have you kept us poor
so that the barbarian in us may arise?

Have you kept us poor
to cause chaos in our midst?
to bring hate in us for one another?
to have us kill each other to survive?

Have you kept us poor?

Have you let this happen?
Have you orchestrated this
so that you can own us?

so that you can break us?
so that you can use us?
so that you might keep your riches?
so that you can drown in power?

while we drowned in sorrows?
Have you kept us poor?

TIME

Oppression can only last for a time
Remember they say
"Time waits for no man"

This means it will surely pass,
and that which comes after
will have questions demanding

Will you get swept away?
Intoxicated by power
Dining on oppression

Will you forget yourself?
Forget there is karma?
Forget that the people aren't airheads?

The people are not animals…and even if they were,
Remember, the rat knows how to survive,
Even in the midst of humans

Leaving you chasing and panting
With brooms, and traps, and sores
And oftentimes, with no win

We may be rats to you
But in time,

you surely will be the panting, losing human

Remember, the jungle has its own humanity
The lion still has to strategize before it hunts
He has to learn to lose, and to survive

Because if all came together in plot
From the mice, giraffes, to the elephants
They'd trample the lion in unity

And yet you are no lion,
Only wide mouth frogs and Tasmanian devils
that don't know when to stop

Do you forget
that if it is stretched enough,
the rubber band will snap?

Do you forget
that even good can come in overdoses?
that there exists a thing like too much water?

If something so vital and necessary
can be detrimental in overdoses,
then what about the bad and poisonous?

You will not be exempt
Your time will come

for oppression only lasts for a time

PUNISHMENT

What is the punishment
for one who takes life arbitrarily?
Dropping skeletons and flesh
in piles of grief and loss

And then sits drunken
with power and potbellies
Enslaving the hope remaining,
of those who come in closure

Boasting of conquests
As though the innocent on the streets of home
were opponents on the enemy's battlefield
Boasting of empty victories

Ending people who faced you
unarmed and singing
in a one-sided battle they had no inkling about
in a one-sided battle they had no power in

'I'll kill you and nothing'll happen'
'I killed him and there's nothing anyone can do'
'Waste him'
bang *bang* *bang* *bang*

Wasting lives and hope

while you watch in satisfaction
Showcasing the heart of evil
as your biggest achievement

What should be the punishment
for one who takes life arbitrarily?
Dropping skeletons and flesh
in piles of grief and loss

Let the dogs tear skin
off your overfed limbs?
Or the birds do same
from your living form?

Dismemberment in slow tide?
Or the ruins of those you love
strewed in gory
right in front of your eyes?

Or some would say mercy
A pardon…or a simple jail term
Would that even be sufficient?
Would that be punishment enough?

HOARDING THE FEED

I adopted a dog
They said don't feed him regularly
For the sake of training him
And I wondered how that was love

You've fancied us your pack of dogs
And you took their advice
Ensuring your power
by ensuring our misery on empty stomachs

We cried for food,
you acted like there was none
You got help from others, got feed for the people
and kept it in your backyards

Throwing at us just enough
Just enough to survive
Just enough to stay waiting and hoping
Just enough to obey

And even when there was a surplus,
you hoarded the feed
Bags in thousands, camping
Rotting away in warehouses

The people starved while you fed on their dues

And when your stomachs could take no more
and you could feed no more,
you saved the rest

And after you stashed away your savings,
there was still so much more
And so you let them rot
so that your hold on us wouldn't rot

Hoarding them for no reason
It would cost you nothing to give them out,
to save the lives of the lifeless
But your quest for power won't permit that

But hear ye today
Power drunk, power hungry men
It can only last for a while
For the people will rise

They say "What doesn't kill you
Makes you stronger", Makes you fearless
Think on that; For if we don't fear a thing,
We can't be threatened by it

The people will get used to hunger
and then you'll lose your hold
The dog you starve into obedience
will one day lose care and do as it pleases

It will fight for itself and get its due
It will rise above your control
After all, hunger is no more a thing to fear
and can no longer be used to control it

That day is near
As we have already seen the beginnings
Hidden palliatives while the people starved
We have risen and taken back what is ours

And we will continue to take back our feed
In whatever form or means
And when you can't provide what you have stolen
You will answer to the hungry dogs

You can control a dog by starving it
But don't cross the line
Else one day it will eat you without heed
You'll be delicious unlimited feed

THE CHOSEN ALTERNATIVE

I pondered silently, questions plaguing me
Guns in my psyche
Gunshots in my ears
It made no sense
Was that the only alternative?

Preying on your children of the soil
Taking away their trust and hope in humanity
by the barrel of your weapons on their pleading bones
Spilling their innocent blood
and watching in disdain while they bleed away

Excuses run amok
Senseless reasons for taking lives that you saw birth
Ignorant rationalities to justify your evil
Defending your atrocities with claims that stank
Claims that stank of illiteracy and laziness

I ponder silently
Are these true reasons?
Or mere diversions and denials
Ways to not accept the truth:
You are lazy entitled fools

Lazy entitled fools handed weapons of destruction
Lazy entitled fools reluctant to hustle

Lazy entitled fools refusing to learn
Lazy entitled fools greedy for what is not theirs
Lazy entitled fools, with no value for life and people

If your victims were truly criminals
If your victims were truly prostituting
If your victims were truly fraudsters
If your victims were truly a menace
Was that the only alternative?

The hand of the law awaits
The consequences of the court call out
The pain of due process sneers at defaulters
You chose not to embrace these calls
But that of the wild beast seeking blood and spoils

Was that the only alternative?
I'll say no
That was not the only alternative
We will all say so
Though you'll say no

But your laziness shies away in fear
Afraid to struggle the way the rest of us do
Afraid you wouldn't survive on your own
Afraid it's too hard for you to make happen
So you prey on those who have

Envy steals their sweat
Envy steals their peace
Greed steals their livelihood
Greed steals their sanity
Your evil stole their lives

Because you chose the path
of the empowered lazy man
Hungry for food and power at all costs
At all costs… illegitimate or not
You chose greed and murder for riches
and not humanity, empathy, and smart work

And yet the criminals walk free
The fraudsters fund your demise
The murderers roam in pomp and pride
While you salute them and pave the way
or run when they challenge your weapons with theirs

Just like guard dogs with no sense of analysis
You'd kill the sweet ones
Those who smiled from their hearts at you
And you'd guard the evil
The evil that steals your future and tramples on you

Make that make sense
But apparently it does to you
Giving your life for them and becoming them

Rather than finding other right ways to survive
From where you sit… or out of those facilities

Afterall, no one tied you down to your offices
Are your uniforms glued to your skins?
Are you word-bound never to leave?
Or are you just lazy men in love with the power rush,
The superiority your weapons make you feel?

So you see
It wasn't the only alternative
But it was the chosen alternative

PATRIOTS...AFTER THE 20

We wept
We fought
We spoke

We broke
We asked
What's next?

Some amongst us gave up
Gave up on our motherland
Gave up on what we called home

Seeking ways to escape
Long before…and now after
Now after the 20

Green booklets
Had lost demand
Had lost significance

Had lost hope
Long before…and now after
Now after the 20

Yet some amongst us
Brave hearts

Our brothers and sisters

Resolved never to leave
Home was theirs,
and they would heal her

The free land…the lands of power
had had their own revolutions
had had their own clinics

And so they vowed that they would heal ours
Make her great again
… if ever she was

And if she ever was…then she would be again
No more long before… but now after
Now after the 20

CORE OF THE WOMAN

They say the woman gets tired of things easily
They say the woman is too emotional
They say the woman is not rational enough
They say politics is not a woman's zone

They say she is weak
She is a secondary citizen
Without a man she is 'weird, incomplete'
They say she should be in 'the other room'

They say she should be 'a woman'
She should know her place
She should not meddle
They say decisions aren't hers to make

But she rose
She spoke
She fought
She rallied

And with her emotions she called the world
With her rational mind she worked the people
With her voice she fought the powers
And with her determination she exposed their wiles

And with her resilience she sprung back

With her bruises she stood firm
With her opened palm, she fed the people
With her fist, she stood for justice

All the women of Nigeria
All the women of Africa
The power of a woman
The core of a woman

They didn't see it
They couldn't grasp it
They disregarded it
They called it weakness and emotions

But with her core, she fought
she pulled hope and love to us
With her breasts, she nurtured
she nurtured us in dire need

And with her essence
She showed us that we can make a difference
She showed us that there will be a future
That there will be a country

I guess you see now
The reason why nature is a woman
The reason why earth is a woman
Mother Earth. Mother Nature. Mother Nurtures

Dedicated to all women
Dedicated to all African women
Dedicated to all Nigerian women
Dedicated to all the women who made a difference 20-10-2020
Specially dedicated to DJ Switch,
Aisha Yesufu,
Feminist.co
Fk abudu

STUPID REVENGE

Why do you fight us?
Why do you take your revenge on us?
The people we chose
to govern and to serve us
They torture you
and you turn and torture us

They take your bread
and juggle with your dignity
They kill your dreams and hope
They manipulate and control you
Turn you to murderers and leave you hanging
and you turn and squash our lives in your hands

Who are you exacting revenge on?
The world?
The true evils?
Or The innocent?
Stupid revenge!
Or is it revenge at all?

Is it revenge at all?
or were you simply always like them
What have the people done to you?
How have the people wronged you?
Or is it corrupted power? Just like your oppressors

Shame on you

Are you so weak and scared?
Scared of the bullies that torment you,
that you run from them
and vent on your wards
Are you so shameless and lost
that you care bout right and wrong no longer?

You let them wield you
You have become the monsters that made you
You are broken men
Turned into dogs of prey by your weakness
Running away from your failures
by embracing beast-hood

Where is your strength
To stand for the right and revolt?
To end your corruption
To find your own voice
To repair your existence
To correct your future

Awaken, ye fools
Raise your incompetent weapons
to the evil that tortures you
Slay them in their sleep
Leave the innocent who suffer beside you

Leave the innocent who fight for you

Awaken, ye fools
Raise your incompetent weapons
to the evil that tortures you
Exact your revenge
and ruin those who wronged you
Ruin those who ruined you

Awaken, ye fools
Fight right
and end your stupid revenge!

HOME AND ABROAD

A people bled and cried in pain
A people lost and lamented
A people staggered and persevered
A people called for help

Who would have thought
that while we fought at home,
we would fight from foreign lands
Home and abroad we merged

While our brothers
While our sisters
were in the land of the foreign,
they raised their fists for us

They screamed in our voices
They recognized their voices in ours
They raised the roof
They kicked the sand

They spoke for us,
As us,
With us,
In us

They spoke so loud the world listened

Spoke so loud the world asked
Spoke so loud the world sympathized
Spoke so loud the world joined in their voices

And while we called on everything
While we called on everyone we could
They did the same
with all they had in them

And we got heads to turn
We got tongues to roll
We got questions to be asked
We got more fists raised in solidarity

And when our necks were squeezed
And our march stifled
And our lives taken
They went on

They kept marching for us
They kept speaking for us
They kept their fists raised
They kept demanding the answers we wanted

Home and abroad we fought
Black spoke from the world afar,
stretching hands in ways they could
We fought as one voice, together

Across the seas, across the skies
Across tribes and languages
Across differences
We fought as one voice together

And as we fought in foreign lands
We grew our family, we expanded
Expanded through the foreigners who stood by us
Through the strangers who held our cause

To us all, at home
To them all, our brothers in diaspora
To them all, the international players
We say thank you

To the famed, who raised their fists in our name
To the John Does, who voiced our pain
To brothers, Home and abroad
We say thank you

THE MILITARY'S WHY

There's questions I ponder
Questions circling the rationale to your actions
Is this really your mandate like they say?

Or is it the lack of victory
The powerlessness and uselessness
that sits within you

Is it a voicelessness and lack of will
that haunts you?
Haunts you to hunt the innocent

Where do your weapons draw the line?
What leads you?
What do you uphold?

Where do your morals and identities draw the line?
To protect and not destroy
Or isn't that what you were created for?

They say you are just pawns in hands
Hands of those who wield your titles and paychecks
Those who give you instructions

Just as we all are pawns
in different walks of life

To the fulfillment of those who fleshen our pockets

But we draw the line
Where our fulfillment meets theirs
And their wishes don't corrupt our souls

Again I ask
Are you simply pawns? blind helpless pawns?
Is that really your mandate like they say?

Or is it the loss of victory?
The powerlessness and uselessness
The voicelessness and lack of will

That sits within you
That haunts you to haunt the innocent
Or is it something else?

RESCUE THE POLICE

Though they have become the enemy
Though they have become the symbol of evil
Though they have started the beginning of the end

They are only tools
Tools used by true evil
Manipulated and oppressed

The police have been punished as well
Starved by the very nation they swore to protect
Framed by the very people they trusted for mandate

The police have been punished as well
Left to rot in poverty
Their families seeking and begging for bread

The police have been punished as well
Left in the scorching sun to patrol
Sent home with scalding skins and empty stomachs

The police have been punished as well
Given sties for schools
And hovels for training grounds

The police have been punished as well
Ordered to shoot to kill innocents

Then thrown under the bus

The police have been punished as well
Forced to commit crimes
And then fed to the peoples revenge

The police have been punished as well
And then set up
at the receiving end of our own swords

The police have been punished as well
People who swore to protect and to serve
Who protects them? Who saves them?

What a shame!
What a pain!
The police have been punished as well

And sadly, they have turned
Turned against the path of right
Turned against us

RECHRISTENING

What happens when I've been a bad child?
What happens when I've stolen something precious?
What happens when I've wronged everyone?
What will mother do?
Scold me or rechristen?

What happens when our uncles and aunties
meant to protect us from a beating
What happens when they beat us, beat us to pulp?
What will mother do?
Restrict them or rechristen?

What happens when our older bother
sent to help us defeat our bullies
What happens when he becomes the bully?
What will mother do?
Punish him or rechristen?

What happens when our older sister
sent by mother to save us from torture
What happens when she becomes the torturer?
What will mother do?
Sentence her, or rechristen?

What happens when our lovers
meant to deepen and complement our peace

What happens when they become our horror?
What will mother do?
Save us or rechristen?

Mother fancies us daft and worthless
Not worth her voice, her care, her ears
Not worth her bother, her efforts, her answers
So she rechristens our poisons
and then goes back to shutting her eyes

Or maybe she is wide-eyed,
and maybe she is orchestrating,
plotting our pain and the shedding of our blood
the tearing of our hearts, and the shredding of our joy
For power drunken mother finds therein her benefits

And so she'll break us all
Kill us all without losing sleep
So she can satisfy her greed and feed
And when we cry out and fight back
She'll rechristen her weapons but retain them

Ill call you David, ill call you Faith
And if you raise your hand to me
Maybe I'll give you a change of clothes
You'll now be known as Joshua,
You'll now be known as Sharon

So, go ahead and make me bleed
I guess that's fine from now on
Because you no more bear the name nigeria
Because you have been rechristened
Because you now bear the name Nigeriah

I guess that makes all the difference
After all, mother teaches us so;
To rechristen our pains
To rechristen your weapons
And continue living the torture

OF LAGOS

How much could one man have
while the hands who feed you starve?
How much can one generation have?
A generation yet to arrive
While there sits houses full of ware
enough for a nation to survive

Where is the humanity?
Even thieves steal for needs
So what is it called
when we steal just because?
When we steal for power
When we steal for greed

How does greed and selfishness
dig so deep into souls
That mere deaths of legion
will put you to peaceful slumber
While the hideous loss of money…so grave a loss
would awaken you to action…So inhumane an action

Stealing from us
in a myriad of ways
Feeding on our sweat,
and then killing us off
when our pleas for life

stop your fund-flow

What point have we reached?
When godfathers with tight fists
remind you with public pomp
that he has the nation in his palms
At what point will we reach?
When will we flush the menaces?

The menaces
…Of lagos

MOTHER SMOTHERS

What will be our stories
when mother presses our necks?
Smiling in our eyes
while she watches the life seep out of us

Strangers stabbed us
They told us we weren't human
We fought them or couldn't care less
After all, they were just strangers

But then we came home
and mother twisted the knife
She put in more blades…in more places
Then sat and laughed

She laughed in our faces as we died
We died of heartbreak and betrayal
More than we died
of blades, blood, and bullets

And in that moment, we realized
That we would rather the strangers suffered us
than watch our death in mother's gleeful eyes
By mother's gleeful hands

We wondered

Was this the devil and the deep blue sea?
Or was it really no dilemma
After-all, mother sold us to the strangers

She had become one and the same
with the opponents we battle
She had become the enemy's muse
She had become the devil and the deep blue sea

Mother, our plague
Mother, who smothers
Mother, who tortures
Mother, our demise

And so a great number of us
learnt to pick the strangers over home
Because they thought it better,
the better torture

For it would make more sense
if a stranger beats us to death
Than if mother silently watches
while we die slow, painful deaths by her gleeful hands

LILLIPUTIAN CITIZENS, PIFFLING OFFICES

You spit on us
With no regard for the seat of power
With no respect for the people and a nation

We demand the answers you owe us
You sit silent, missing in action
Not batting an eyelash

And even when recorders face you
Your words drip with absentmindedness
Beautifully laced with stupidity

If you really are incompetent
Then why not sit at home like the masses
and leave the service for the capable

Save us the communal shame
Downright disrespect for the people
Sheer disregard for office

Officials strutting public media
Exalting themselves
Self-ordaining with titles of lordship

The arrant insult of coordinating your evildoers
In broad daylight, while we watched

To do your dirty deeds of destruction

The arrant insult of running down a nation
Stealing from the masses for pleasure
and killing them when they cry

The arrant insult of a firing squad
Right before our eyes
With no fear or worries

Impunity is the word
Impunity you have created and ensured
Impunity that takes away our respect due

So you don't do due diligence
You don't learn governance
And you perambulate through speech and service

By what means did you get there?
How did you come by your responsibilities?
Surely not merit

For if twas merit
You'd have an equipping, a respect
You'd have a reasoning

A presence of mind, a concern
Informed and well thought out answers

You'd fear your shortcomings

And if you feel no wariness
at failing the nation, failing us
You'd be wary

Wary of losing what you earned
Wary of losing the people and their support
Wary for your own dignity and sake

But merit had no part to play, did it?
Worthiness had no hand, did it?
Deceit and manipulation sealed your win

You serpented your way in there
And now rule with impunity
With incompetence and self-service

The people didn't matter
For they are simply Lilliputians
And the offices are piffling to you

KARMA

They say karma is a b****
But I wonder if that's true
Is she really a merciless c***?

And I wonder when she's a b****
Does she always come?
Or does she sometimes forget?

Will she visit you
In your own lifetime?
Wouldn't it be a career failure if she didn't?

Well, I wont wait to find out
For you could be gone peacefully before she comes
So Ill help her out, just in case

Call me Karma, Ill be a b****
Ill make her dreams come true,
Execute her job better

And ill make you pay
For every single sin
For every single wrong

Sit with me, Lets have a chat
How would you love your wages

In kind, or in kind?

Broken fingers first
or severed limbs first
Where do we start?

Do we burn your loved ones?
Or do we spare them,
but make them watch?

Maybe visit the ancient practices of China
Explore the breathtaking Lingchi
and bask in the beautiful sight of your blood?

I've always been a fan of the creativity in rat torture
Gnawing its way through you
in desperation for its life…and maybe food

Hey, how about a big beautiful pot of cool water
Would you like to sit in that
While we turn up the heat to boiling point?

How long would you last?
How loud would you cry?
Watching your own demise like you watched ours

That's a more merciful wage
I'm trying to be sweet

And maybe a little lenient

Oh Karma, you really are a b****
A punctual one serving justice
You can call me Karma, 'cause I do it better

10

CAN'T GO BACK

The clock just turned
Striking a revolution
The difference has come
An awakening we see

Some may speak of a failure
We may be disheartened in the wake of our pain
Feel hopeless in the wake of our horror
We may have no inkling, what's next, we say

But a truth I offer
Should diffuse the tension in our hearts
Permeate past the grief and soreness,
and open our teary eyes to promises

I promise the certainty of a better tomorrow
For our children, and perhaps for us
For this is just the beginning
of things to come, better things

Unity, Empathy, love, humanity
Equity, Women empowerment, justice, selflessness
Wealth, craft, creativity, liberty
Loyalty, individualism, comfort, belonging

And amongst others

A voice, one voice, the national voice
One that counts. One that is heard
One that makes the difference

A reality we have not known
But we are now creating
But we have now created
That our children will see, and maybe even us

Mourn your lost and losses
Then dry your eyes in comfort
For we didn't fight in vain
and can never go back to what we were

THE POOR WILL DEFINITELY EAT

If the poor don't eat today while you do
One day will come, they say
And "the poor shall eat the rich"

If they don't eat today while you do
With smiles on their faces
With merry and as a family

They'll eat tomorrow
After you have been in the kitchen
After you have cooked

But you won't be wearing aprons and hats
You won't be serving, my dear
For you will be a course

Oh yes, the poor shall eat
One day, no matter what
This is a truth

But I fear, I have a question
Who will be the meal?
The rich or the middle class

Whatever your answers may be
It will truly be a massacre

A massacre for us all, I fear

For the concept of rich and poor,
middle and elite classes
may be chaotic in the mind of the uneducated

The hand of poverty
can blur the lines
and you may get cut down regardless

The anger and hate in poverty
doesn't often care for society levels
Simply having more is enough eligibility

One day the poor will eat the rich
But will the middle class accompany
as a simple snack or dessert to complete the meal?

Whatever your answers may be
It will truly be a massacre
A massacre for us all, I fear

So speak up as you can
Lets win together
Or eat the rich together…in the least

HOLD THE BORDERS OF OUR HOPE

If you march home
with hands empty and loss lingering
Let not your heads and hearts
be empty

What you have witnessed
What you have been a part of
is a mark of the future
A scar of beautiful things to come

Unity amongst brothers
and discord infiltrating the enemy's ranks
Telling tales of beginning times
Telling tales of a revolution unevaded

Tis the knowledge we now have
The stirring in our hearts
that things will never be the same
because we know and have seen

You can be heard;
When your voices are louder
When your hands are stronger
together as one

Educate you

Raise your children in this knowledge
Tis like they say 'United we stand
Divided we fall'

So hold the borders of our hope
Hold them tight and hold them down
Let not the walls crumble
For hope is all we have

Tis all we have
and twill birth a revolution

AN IDENTITY IN REEDUCATION

The identity of a people
A discussion to be had
Reforms to be made

Greed stirs within the average individual
What is the rationale with which we operate?
Where is the love?

While we fight and blame the head
The middle stinks
The bottom is rotting

Why do we fight ourselves?
Why do we dwell on division?
Are we not one skin, one nation?

Where lies the definition of your identity?
Where lies the recognition of your being?
Where lies the recognition of kindred?

Is it purely in location and geography?
Is it purely in lingo?
Is it purely in tradition?

The cabbie who takes too many turns
So the hustler can pay more

All because you took a ride

The employer who enslaves the worker
Milking them like machines
All because you pay his bills

The mother who abuses her kin
In different ways, ways that we accept
All because…African parents

The ones who scorn him from the other tribe
They say they are better
All because he's from another room in the national
home

The rape apologist and enabler
who blames women for their victimization
All because of what they wore

Lets play a game of truth
The abused infants and women in hijabs
What then was their crime?

The seller who empties your pockets with pride
Even though you're just trying to survive as well
All because times are hard

The evils in uniforms

Who loot your sweat
and shoot your brains out

Who shed your blood
Shatter dreams and futures
with myopic reasons

The say your hair and possessions scream 'shoot me'
All because life has smiled on your hard work
Is that not ignorance or yes?

The online vendor can't deliver for fear of her life
in an unstable state with blood being shed,
and drivers looted on the streets

The buyer in homestay, doesn't give a hoot
Demands her package immediately for her event,
so the vendor offers a pickup location

Now the buyer can't come for fear of her life
in an unstable state with blood being shed
and drivers looted on the streets

Where is the humanity? Where is the love?
We all say 'na street', 'na hustle'
We say "na condition cause am"

We say" na government cause am"

We say 'na naija we dey'
We say, I say 'na naija we dey'

But while we fight the government
Shamelessly, we have become little governments,
to different depths, for different reasons

Regardless, we must fight
For we must begin somewhere
A reeducation is what we need

Of the average man and sundry
Down to the roots, up to the top
Sideways and all ways

An identity in Reeducation

UNITY

One language, one tribe
One location, one identity
One people, one demand
Thus, was our unity

For what is tribe
once past geography and culture?
What is culture
once past simply repeated practices?

What is language
once past words and letters?
And what is religion
once past love and redemption?

Life is paramount
Humanity is key
Catering to us all
Under one umbrella

Giving us peaceful factions
of one shared umbrella
Shading us all, from harsh rays of the sun
and brutal pellets of the rain

Unity

Was the language we spoke
Was the religion we practiced
Was the culture we practiced

Unity
Was the location we chose
Was our voice
And will be our savior

THERE WILL BE A COUNTRY

There will be a country
Like there was a country
We rest, after the test
but you haven't seen yet our best

Our children will enjoy the fruits
of a nation so true
So true to its people
that it would hurt to seem them cripple

Our children will own a country so proud,
and not this one wrapped in a shroud
They will suckle on the breasts of a nation,
one with milk that brings life and not death

A nation governed by true compatriots
Nigeria's call obey,
building a nation, a home, a refuge
An identity of humanity and family.

There will be a country
Strong as we once were
It'll take years, tears and blood
But there will be a country

A country our hearts yearn for

A country we wear with pride
A country like our fathers once saw…and better
There will be a country

EDUCATION FOR US ALL

Let it be known
The power of education
The value of education
For us all

Education for us;
The old and grey
Education for the future;
Our sons and daughters

Education in and out of boxed halls and school fields
Education in the field of life;
from morals and visionaries,
from humanity and maturity

Education for power and clarity
to see the truth and the ways otherwise cloaked
Cloaked by a web of poverty and manipulation,
luring us to our demise through ignorance

Education for understanding
Understanding that strengthens us to see the truth
To see what benefits
and to see what ruins

To stand for what is right

To be not swayed or deceived
by ignorance or by poverty
Let it be known the value of education

THE GIANT OF AFRICA

The Giant of Africa
is what we are called
For so long a dishonored crown
For we were nothing close to giants,
much less THE giant

Wallowing in self-mutilation
Creating monsters from our very core
Monsters made from the squalor and oppression,
unsparingly meted out by our fathers
through a system that corrupted

A system that turned hearts;
From that of the innocent love-filled babe
to that of the howling wolf in the night
Seeking prey with no remorse or thought,
and devouring the innocent for survival sake

And so we were less than giants
We scrambled, begged, and sought livelihood
We fought foreign forces and we fought homely forces
We became the monsters that made us
and we were the monsters we fought

But then a time came when we became one
Ignoring the petty divides that broke us

Religion, location, language,
We held hands as one, united in misery and pain
…and the world heard us

And as our cries came louder
Waves of strength and hope reverberated
Through the continent, to brothers and sisters
Through our melanin, to fighters and heroes
Through love, to the very heart of Mama Africa

The Giant of Africa stood
Broken, wailing, hurting, and winning
Screaming, braving, fighting, and surviving
Dying, sorrowing, fearing, and upholding
And the continent fed on her power

The Giant of Africa
began the journey to its crown
Becoming a power house
Sending strength through Africa
Sending hope that Africa will stand again

A MIRAGE OF EMPATHY

We are all lumps of flesh and bones
Skeletons walking and surviving
All feeble and brittle
All lost in one second
That's how deep our strength goes

Cept for the souls we carry
The core we hold on to
The bane of our existence
The beauty of our existence
Salient above all

The demise of the flesh is horrific
Irreparable flesh bleeding to the ground
Lifeless blood torn and shredded
Screams and tears, Brokenness and pain
A horror to behold and a horror in its wake

But the demise of the soul
Slow, silent, abrupt or without drama
Is the icing on the cake
Crowning the heartbreak
Crowning the horror

Souls slowly losing hold
Eyes draping closed for eternity

Beautiful loves and smiles gone to come no more
Hopes dashed in the sand
Children lost in the arms of mothers

Now the memories of the ones we loved,
memories of the ones we had
sadly haunt us, never to leave
We cry in the dark as we yearn for their touch
We cry in the crowd as we mourn for their tomorrow

A tomorrow shattered
A today shredded
by another just like me
Another who's built his own tomorrow
Where is the empathy?

Here is where humanity visits,
saving souls and flesh
If not for all else,
for the simple sake of likeness
The simple sake that they are you…and you are they

A reality we thought we saw
We knew ought to be
But a reality that was an illusion
We only saw what they wanted us to see
And then what we hoped to see

For such was not the case
Instead, humans who fear pain and ruin
usher ruin and herald pain
What sense did it make
that empathy is only a mirage?

And now we mourn
We mourn the reality that is the truth
One we have to face
A sick one alas
A rotten state of existence

You don't have to love us
You don't have to know our histories
You don't have to know us
You don't have to understand our souls
or agree with our identities

All you have to do is see yourself in my stead
See you where I lay, bleeding
See you where I lay, screaming
See you where I lay, hopeless
See you where I lay, essence slipping away

Because it could be you
Because it could be your mothers and fathers
Because it will be your sons
Because Empathy should not be so far from a human

INDIVIDUALISM

Let this be a lesson in individualism
You'll ask…maybe
What be that?
Ill tell you in a promise

I promise to teach my loved ones
I promise to teach my friends and family
I promise to teach my children
to dwell in the art of individualism

To live by the tenets of individualism
Simply revolving around the individual;
Of self, and of others
Ill tell you why in explanation

He who learns to value the individual person
Seeing through the assumptions of groups
Seeing through the coagulation of groups
to the toils and joys of the single individual

Is he who has begun a journey
A journey to the best possible satisfaction
Best possible satisfaction for all,
founded on recognition of a person's humane needs

Love isn't purely in lingo

Love isn't purely in tradition and groups
Love isn't purely in location and geography
Love is pure in loving the human

In loving the collective
like you would love the individual
In listening to the collective
like you would listen to the individual

Whence a man understands the needs of humans
The needs of individuals
There lies the beginning of empathy
There lies the beginning of communal sharing

For he sees himself as an individual
in his brother the individual
Cares for his brother the individual
as he cares for himself an individual

And hurts for his brother
when he is deprived
of the simple joys
that he himself seeks as a person

I was raised not to see tribe
I was raised not to see location
I was raised not to see language
I was raised to see the person, the individual

From there begins family and empathy
From there begins understanding and care
From there begins love across the borders of tags
Across the borders of divisions that don't matter

Let this be a lesson in individualism
I promise to teach my loved ones
I promise to teach my children
To dwell in the art of individualism

See the person, see the people, see the groups
As individuals with same needs as you
Love, life, hope, homes, joy, health
Care for him, care for them

Care, knowing what the individual needs
Care, as you would for self,
Individualism
Above all else

2020
A NOTE TO THE FUTURE

2020

This is a letter to the future
A note to our children

There was a country
Then there was a joke
A simple scam of a nation
A sham was what we lived

But a time came
As a time will always come
And there was an uprising
As there will always be

The new generation heralded it
Tired of the horror we lived
Tired of the oppression by our own
Ready for our voices to be heard

The results may be debated in the present
But it is my believe that we have reset
Something that was amiss and waiting
For a force to nudge the sleeping beast

The results may be debated
But make no mistake
To think that we have not conquered

To think that we have lost

For we have not
There were no losses
Except for the blood that was shed
We went home with battle wounds and lessons

Lessons for another day
Lessons for another fight
Lessons for the past, our fathers
Lessons for the future, our children, you

For they heard our voice
and their behinds itched in fear
Fear of the fire that approached
Fire that will remold them or destroy them

They were forced to listen
They were forced to move
They were forced to fear
They were forced to fight back

It may seem like a turn for the worse
But when you bother the enemy
So much that it finds you worthy of a fight
That's a victory in itself

Because now we see

Because now we know
That if we stand and fight
We can make a change

If we stand and raise our fists in peace and war
If we stand and raise our voices loud enough
Our voices will be heard
Just as they have been heard

Our voices were heard as one
And though we limp and we hurt
Though we retreat for the moment
We have started a revolution in hearts

We have planted the knowledge of our power
In our minds
In our heads
And in our hands

And that revolution will come to full term
And it shall come to fruition
We will rise again in justice
We will be back fully fortified

And that comeback may be us
And that comeback may take a while
And that comeback may be you
But it will surely come

So in this note, I tell you
We have and will continue to conquer,
Together with and through you
Now and in your time

The future you live now
Was created by us,
By the past, your fathers
By our voices

Remember that
And when it is going downhill again,
Stands up and fight
Because your voice matters and will be heard